REALLY EASY PIANO

DUETS

CHART HITS

WISE PUBLICATIONS
PART OF THE MUSIC SALES GROUP
LONDON / NEW YORK / PARIS / SYDNEY / COPENHAGEN / BERLIN / MADRID / HONG KONG / TOKYO

ALSO AVAILABLE IN THE REALLY EASY PIANO SERIES...

ABBA
25 GREAT HITS. ORDER NO. AM980430

CHILDREN'S FAVOURITES
20 POPULAR HITS. ORDER NO. AM998745

CHRISTMAS
24 FESTIVE CHART HITS. ORDER NO. AM980496

CLASSICAL FAVOURITES
24 WELL-KNOWN FAVOURITES. ORDER NO. AM993366

COLDPLAY
20 SONGS FROM COLDPLAY. ORDER NO. AM989593

ELTON JOHN
24 CLASSIC SONGS. ORDER NO. AM987844

FRANK SINATRA
21 CLASSIC SONGS. ORDER NO. AM987833

GREAT FILM SONGS
22 BIG FILM HITS. ORDER NO. AM993344

GREAT SHOWSTOPPERS
20 POPULAR STAGE SONGS. ORDER NO. AM993355

JAZZ GREATS
22 JAZZ FAVOURITES. ORDER NO. AM1000857

LOVE SONGS
22 CLASSIC LOVE SONGS. ORDER NO. AM989582

MICHAEL JACKSON
19 CLASSIC HITS. ORDER NO. AM1000604

MORE 21ST CENTURY HITS
21 POPULAR HITS. ORDER NO. AM996534

MOZART
22 CLASSICAL FAVOURITES. ORDER NO. AM1000648

NEW CHART HITS
19 BIG CHART HITS. ORDER NO. AM996523

NO. 1 HITS
22 POPULAR CLASSICS. ORDER NO. AM993388

POP HITS
22 GREAT SONGS. ORDER NO. AM980408

SHOWSTOPPERS
24 STAGE HITS. ORDER NO. AM982784

TV HITS
25 POPULAR HITS. ORDER NO. AM985435

60S HITS
25 CLASSIC HITS. ORDER NO. AM985402

70S HITS
25 CLASSIC SONGS. ORDER NO. AM985413

80S HITS
25 POPULAR HITS. ORDER NO. AM985424

90S HITS
24 POPULAR HITS. ORDER NO. AM987811

50 FABULOUS SONGS
FROM POP SONGS TO CLASSICAL THEMES. ORDER NO. AM999449

50 GREAT SONGS
FROM POP SONGS TO CLASSICAL THEMES. ORDER NO. AM995643

50 HIT SONGS
FROM POP HITS TO JAZZ CLASSICS. ORDER NO. AM1000615

PIANO TUTOR
FROM FIRST STEPS TO PLAYING IN A WIDE
RANGE OF STYLES — FAST!. ORDER NO. AM996303

ALL TITLES CONTAIN BACKGROUND NOTES FOR EACH SONG PLUS
PLAYING TIPS AND HINTS.

PUBLISHED BY
WISE PUBLICATIONS
14-15 BERNERS STREET, LONDON, W1T 3LJ, UK.

EXCLUSIVE DISTRIBUTORS:
MUSIC SALES LIMITED
DISTRIBUTION CENTRE, NEWMARKET ROAD, BURY ST EDMUNDS,
SUFFOLK, IP33 3YB, UK.
MUSIC SALES PTY LIMITED
LEVEL 4, LISGAR HOUSE, 30-32 CARRINGTON STREET,
SYDNEY, NSW 2000 AUSTRALIA

ORDER NO. AM1011428
ISBN 978-1-78558-235-6
THIS BOOK © COPYRIGHT 2016 BY WISE PUBLICATIONS,
A DIVISION OF MUSIC SALES LIMITED.

MUSIC ARRANGED BY BARRIE CARSON TURNER.
EDITED BY JENNI NOREY.
PRINTED IN THE EU.

YOUR GUARANTEE OF QUALITY
AS PUBLISHERS, WE STRIVE TO PRODUCE EVERY BOOK TO THE HIGHEST
COMMERCIAL STANDARDS. THE MUSIC HAS BEEN FRESHLY ENGRAVED AND
THE BOOK HAS BEEN CAREFULLY DESIGNED TO MINIMISE AWKWARD PAGE
TURNS AND TO MAKE PLAYING FROM IT A REAL PLEASURE.
PARTICULAR CARE HAS BEEN GIVEN TO SPECIFYING ACID-FREE, NEUTRAL-
SIZED PAPER MADE FROM PULPS WHICH HAVE NOT BEEN ELEMENTAL
CHLORINE BLEACHED. THIS PULP IS FROM FARMED SUSTAINABLE FORESTS
AND WAS PRODUCED WITH SPECIAL REGARD FOR THE ENVIRONMENT.
THROUGHOUT, THE PRINTING AND BINDING HAVE BEEN PLANNED TO
ENSURE A STURDY, ATTRACTIVE PUBLICATION WHICH SHOULD GIVE YEARS
OF ENJOYMENT. IF YOUR COPY FAILS TO MEET OUR HIGH STANDARDS,
PLEASE INFORM US AND WE WILL GLADLY REPLACE IT.

WWW.MUSICSALES.COM

DUETS

CHART HITS

Secondo
All Of Me

Words & Music by John Legend & Tobias Gad

This simple but effective piano- and vocal-based song hit the No. 1 spot in several countries, including the US, Australia, Ireland and Canada. It was written for John Legend's then-fiancé Chrissy Teigen, who he married in 2013. The video shows clips from the couple's honeymoon.

Primo

All Of Me

Words & Music by John Legend & Tobias Gad

Hints & Tips: Set a metronome going and listen to the tempo first, so you know how fast the crotchets need to be. The melody is expressive and should be played smooth and flowing.

Secondo

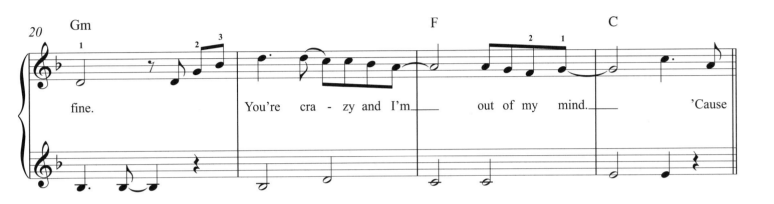

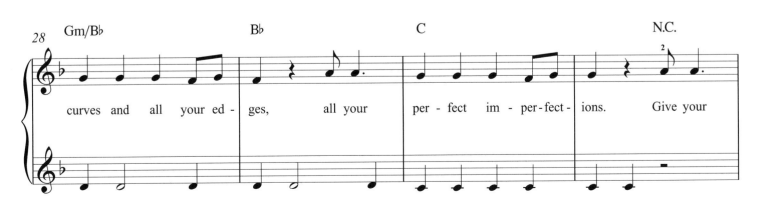

Secondo

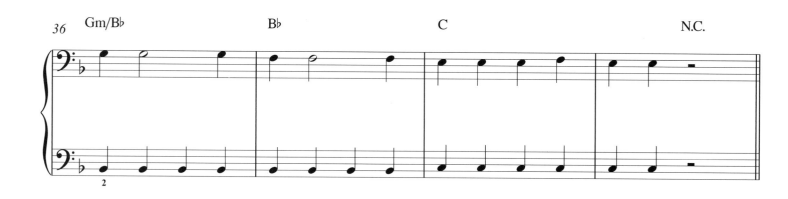

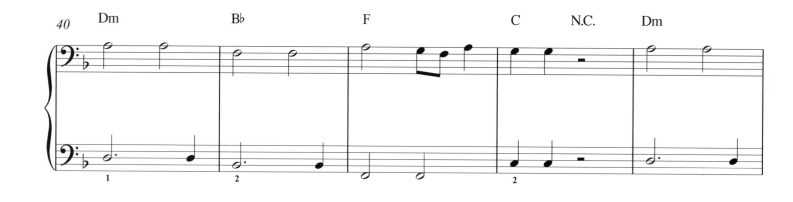

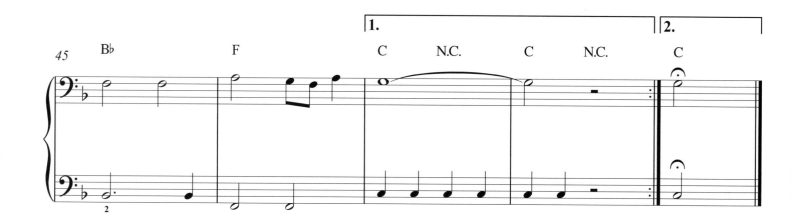

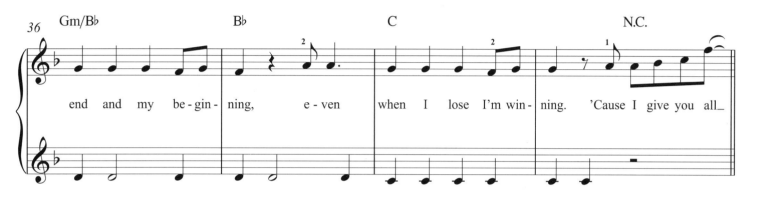

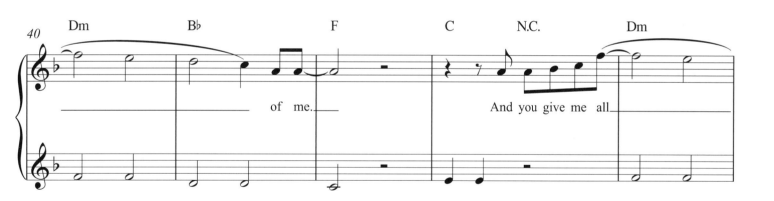

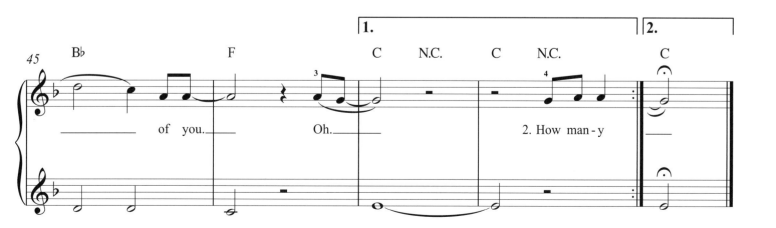

Secondo

Bills

**Words & Music by Jacob Hindlin, Eric Frederic,
Rickard Goransson & Gamal Lewis**

Rocketing from relative unknown to No. 2 on the UK singles chart, Gamal 'LunchMoney' Lewis composed this unusually catchy hit in just 30 minutes. The song's co-writer Ricky Reed (aka Eric Frederic) stated that he wanted to do a modern twist on the gospel rag, combining an ingenious piano riff with electronic drums and production. The infectious chorus and funny lyrics make this the first pop hit for newcomer LunchMoney Lewis.

Primo
Bills

**Words & Music by Jacob Hindlin, Eric Frederic,
Rickard Goransson & Gamal Lewis**

Hints & Tips: The second part plays a big role in this, providing the funky feel for the song! Be sure this part can be played confidently before playing both parts together. The right-hand rhythms from bar 9 are quite fast. To avoid them blurring together, play slightly detached (*staccato*).

Secondo

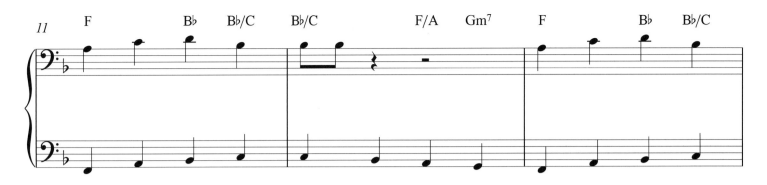

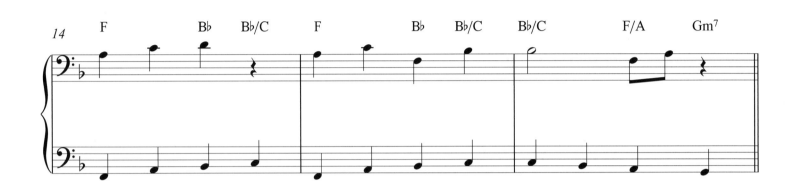

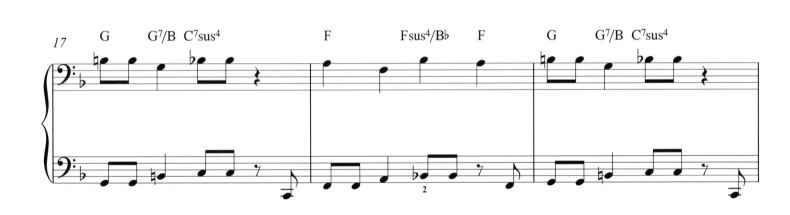

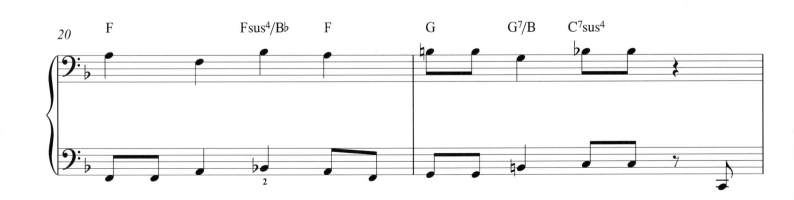

Secondo

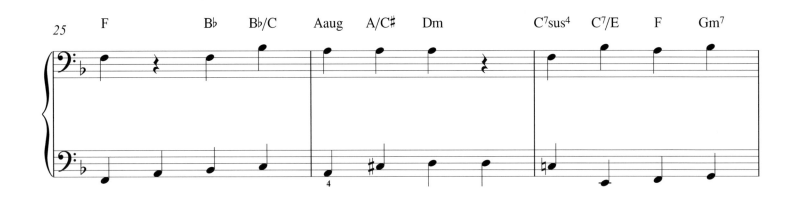

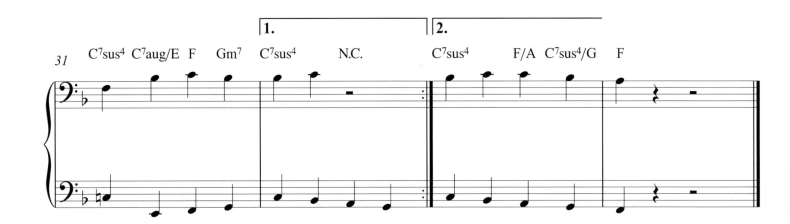

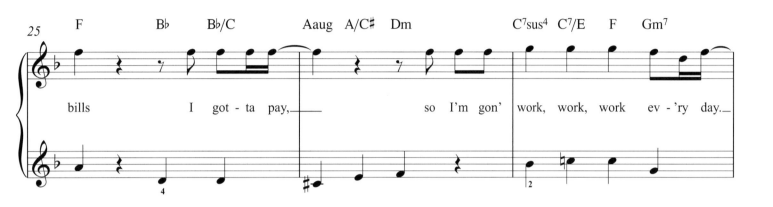

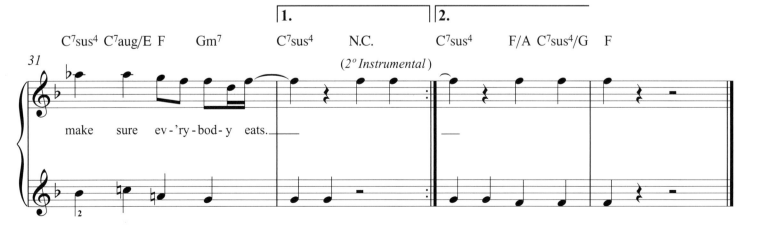

Secondo

Black Magic

**Words & Music by Edvard Erfjord, Henrik Michelsen,
Camille Purcell & Edward Drewett**

'Black Magic', the lead single from Little Mix's third album *Get Weird*, spent three weeks at the top of the UK charts. The supernatural-themed video is set in an American high school and shows the girls playing different characters, which is a break from their usual videos involving singing and dancing.

Primo

Black Magic

Words & Music by Edvard Erfjord, Henrik Michelsen,
Camille Purcell & Edward Drewett

Hints & Tips: Get to grips with the repetitive rhythm in the right hand of the second part first. In bars 10 and 18 of the first part, watch out for the change of hand position in the right hand.

Secondo

18

Primo

19

Secondo

Don't Stop

Words & Music by Stephen Robson, Michael Busbee, Luke Hemmings, Calum Hood & Mark David Stewart

Written as something of an anti-bullying campaign after one of the band members announced on Twitter that his sister was being picked on at school, the video for 'Don't Stop' sees the Australian four-piece dressed as super heroes trying to do good deeds.

Don't Stop

**Words & Music by Stephen Robson, Michael Busbee,
Luke Hemmings, Calum Hood & Mark David Stewart**

Hints & Tips: This is a fun song so try to keep both parts light. Keep crotchets steady in the second part and don't be tempted to speed up, especially in the chorus (from bar 17).

Secondo

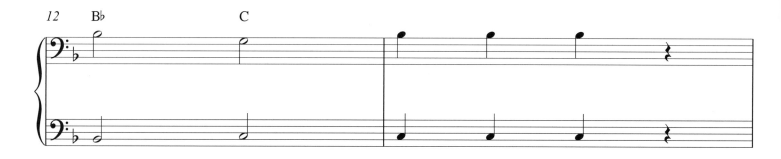

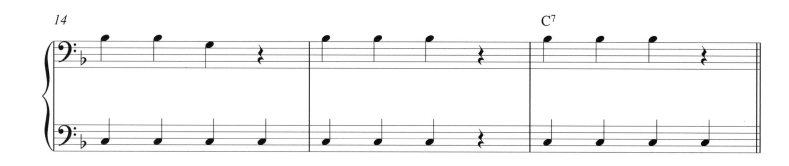

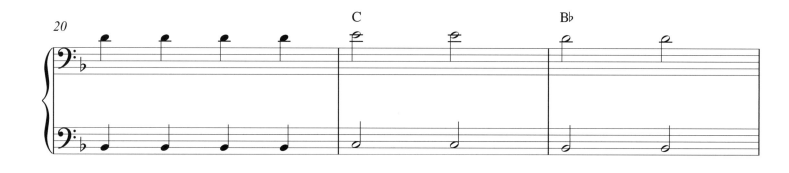

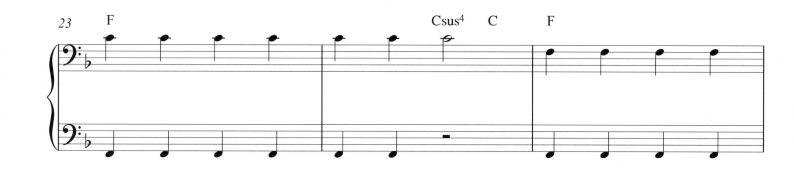

Secondo

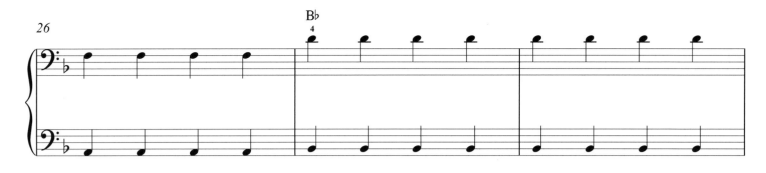

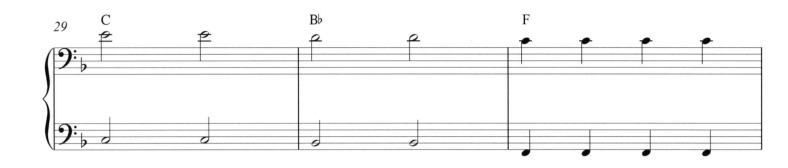

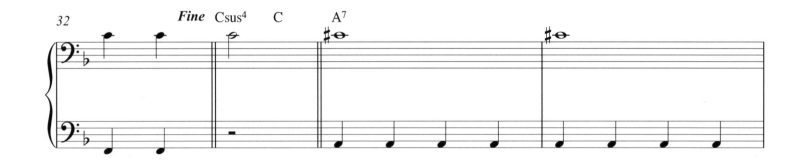

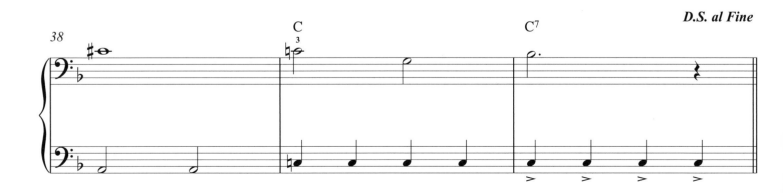

Primo

Secondo
Drag Me Down

Words & Music by John Ryan, Jamie Scott & Julian Bunetta

The first song released after One D member Zayn left the group, 'Drag Me Down' was played 4.75 million times worldwide on its release, breaking the Spotify record for most streams in a single day. It features on band's fifth studio album, *Made In The A.M.*

Drag Me Down

Words & Music by John Ryan, Jamie Scott & Julian Bunetta

Hints & Tips: Take note of the structure before you begin, marking on the *D.S.* and the repeats, so neither player gets lost.

Secondo

30

Primo

Secondo

Flashlight

**Words & Music by Jason Moore, Sia Furler,
Sam Smith, Christian Guzman & Mario Mejia**

'Flashlight' is a downtempo ballad that was composed for the soundtrack of *Pitch Perfect 2* collaboratively by pop powerhouses Sia, Sam Smith, Christian Guzman and Jason Moore. Jessie J's performance is strong and note-perfect, unleashing the passionate vocals for which she has come to be known. The song works perfectly as the emotional climax of the movie, while the music video sees Jessie J visiting the film's fictional university to perform.

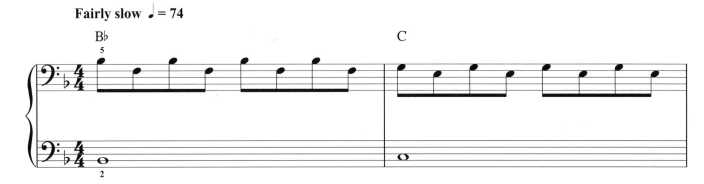

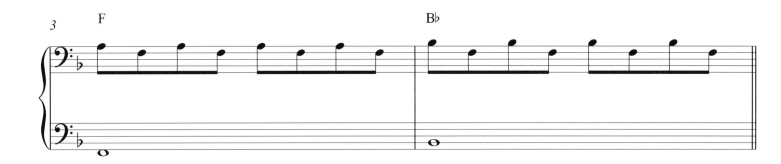

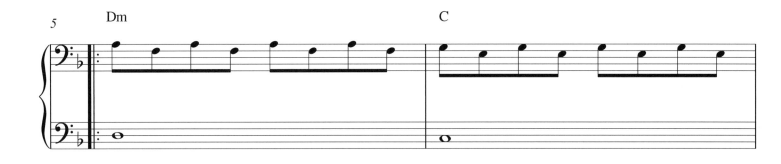

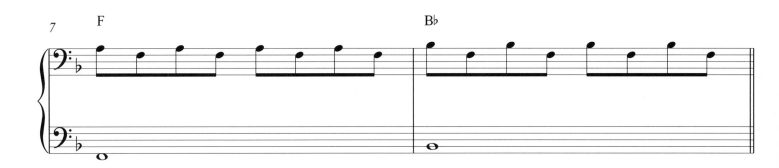

Primo
Flashlight

**Words & Music by Jason Moore, Sia Furler,
Sam Smith, Christian Guzman & Mario Mejia**

Hints & Tips: Keep the left-hand quavers in the second part steady and even. This should help the first-part player to place the semiquavers in the melody.

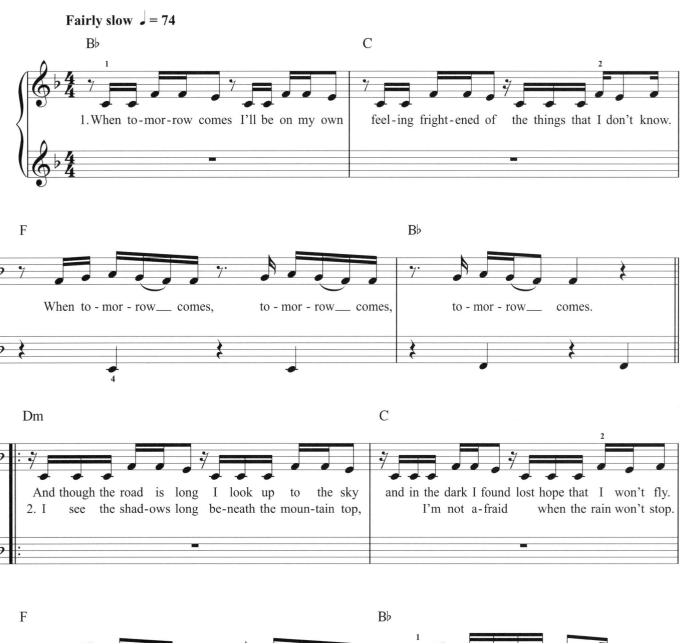

Secondo

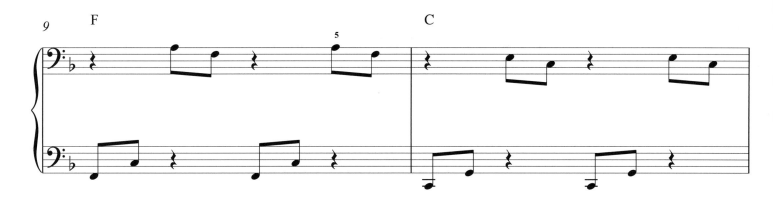

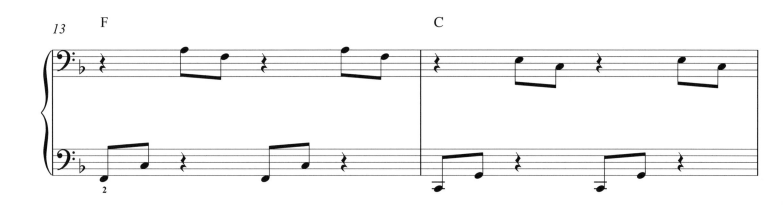

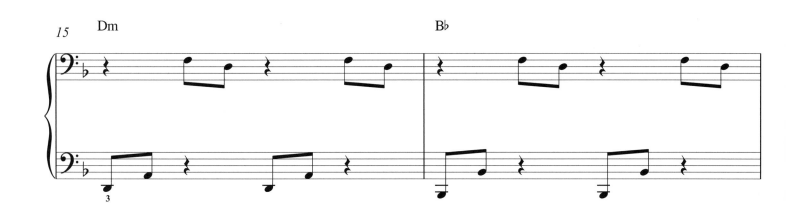

Primo

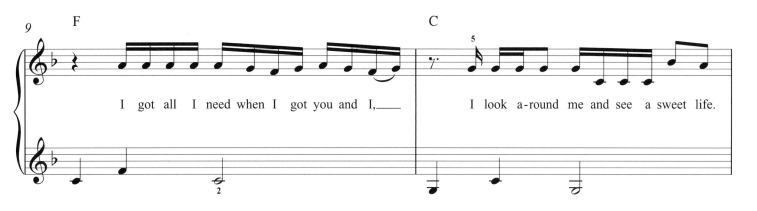

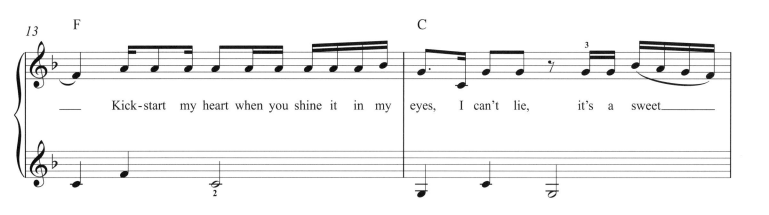

Secondo

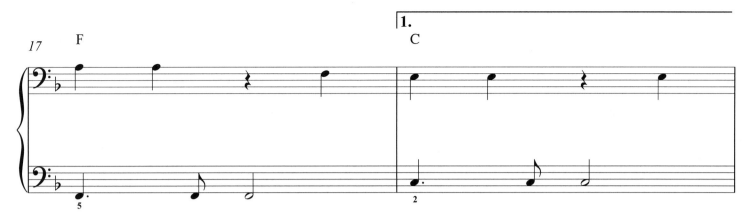

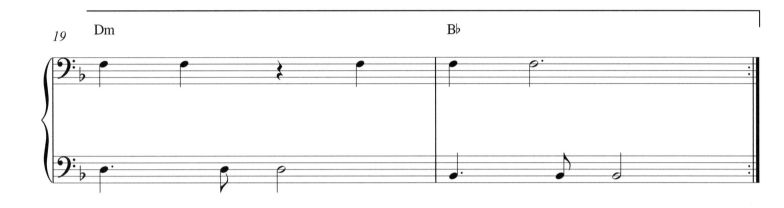

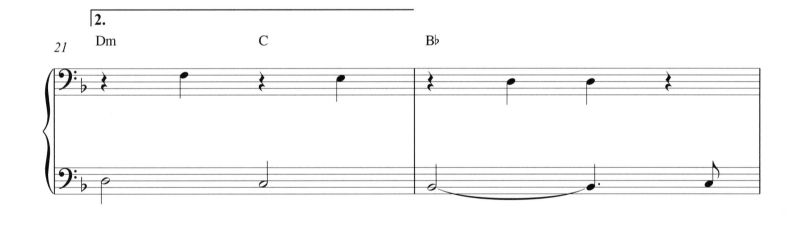

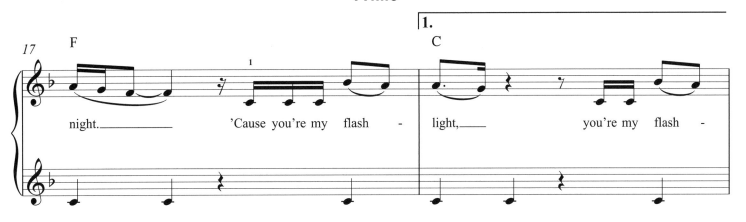

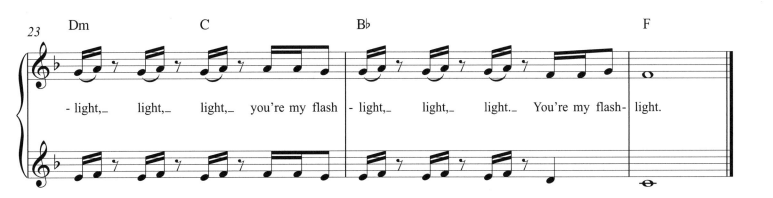

Secondo

Heartbeat Song

**Words & Music by Kara Dioguardi, James Adkins, Thomas Linton,
Richard Burch, Zachary Lind, Audra Butts, Jason Evigan & Allan Mitch**

Opening Kelly Clarkson's 2015 album *Piece By Piece*, 'Heartbeat Song' is a return to her upbeat pop brilliance, after her last single release in 2013. During this period away from music, Clarkson got married and had her first child. The optimistic tone of the lyrics works perfectly together with the uptempo electropop rhythm that is based on the actual heartbeat of her child.

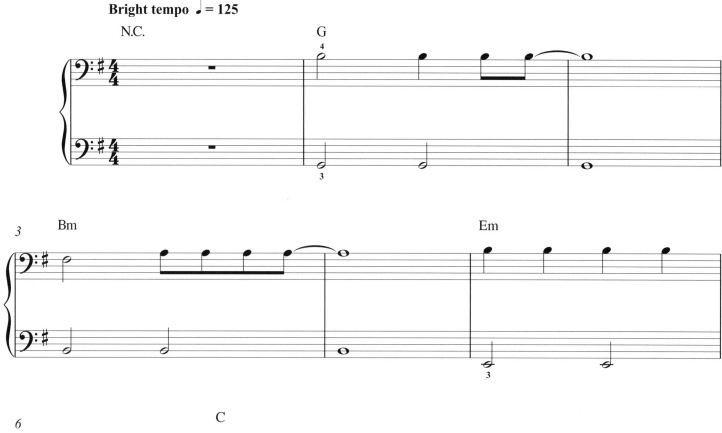

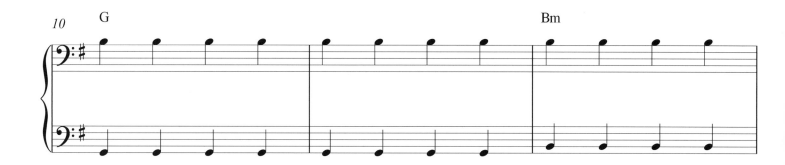

Heartbeat Song

**Words & Music by Kara Dioguardi, James Adkins, Thomas Linton,
Richard Burch, Zachary Lind, Audra Butts, Jason Evigan & Allan Mitch**

Hints & Tips: There's lots of syncopation in the melody, but the steady rhythms in the rest of the parts should
give you a reference for where the main beats of the bar fall.

Secondo

40

Primo

Secondo

Primo

Secondo

Hold Back The River

Words & Music by Iain Archer & James Bay

Opening the second single from James Bay's album is a quiet guitar riff that opens up a heartfelt verse before giving way to the anthemic chorus. According to Bay, the song is about the feeling of being unable to see friends and family during a busy touring and recording schedule. After winning the Critics' Choice award at the Brits 2015 and seeing his album hit No. 1 in the UK Chart, his diary was so demanding that he welcomed the opportunity to finally see his friends and family.

Primo

Hold Back The River

Words & Music by Iain Archer & James Bay

Hints & Tips: Watch out at the start, as both parts are playing the same rhythm but different notes. Keep it steady and precise.

Secondo

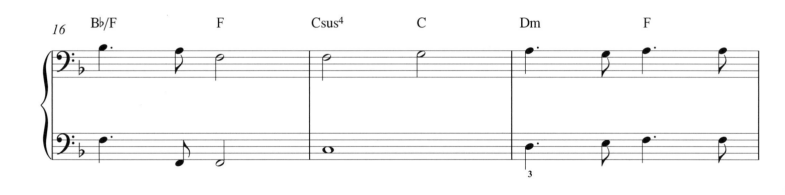

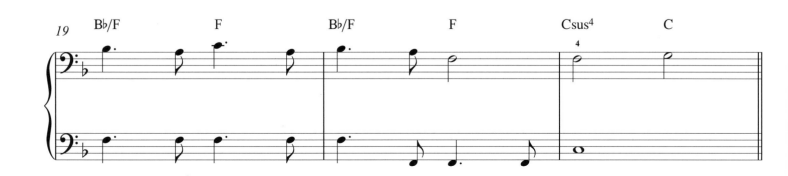

for a min-ute and___ see where you___ hide. Hold back the riv - er, hold back.___

Once up - on a diff - 'rent life we

rode our bikes in-to the sky.___ But now we crawl a -

- gainst the tide. Those dis - tant days are flash-ing by.___

Secondo

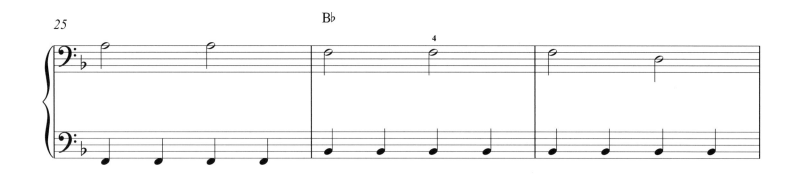

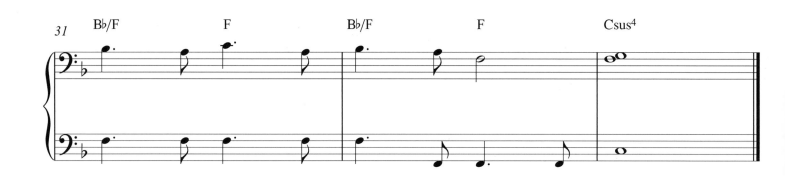

Secondo

I Really Like You

**Words & Music by Peter Svensson, Carly Rae Jepsen
& Jacob Hindlin**

Reportedly, when making plans for her third album *Emotion*, Carly Rae Jepsen's manager told her she couldn't release anything unless it was on the level of her biggest hit 'Call Me Maybe'. She then released this danceable pop number 'I Really Like You', whose chorus ensures it'll go down in pop history. The lyrics are about being in a relationship where it's just too soon to say "I love you".

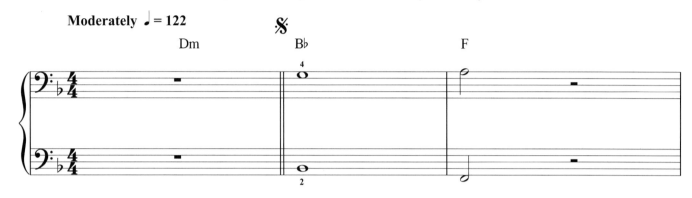

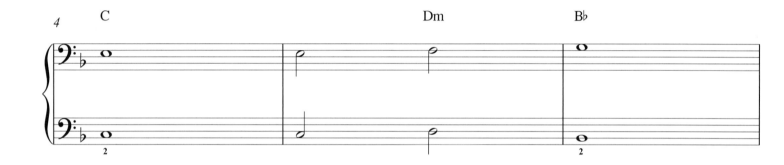

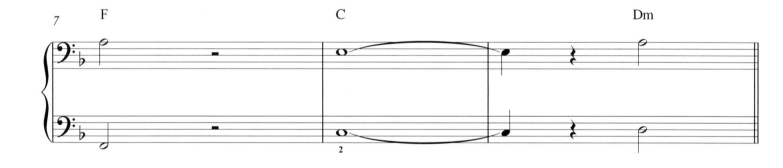

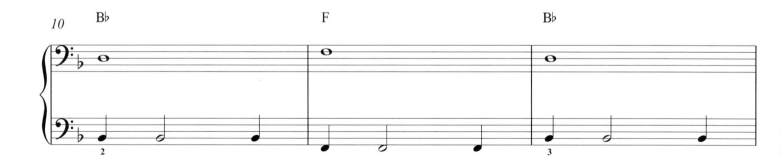

Primo
I Really Like You

**Words & Music by Peter Svensson, Carly Rae Jepsen
& Jacob Hindlin**

Hints & Tips: The first-part player should check over the fingering in bars 18 and 19, as this is the trickiest bit
in the piece.

Secondo

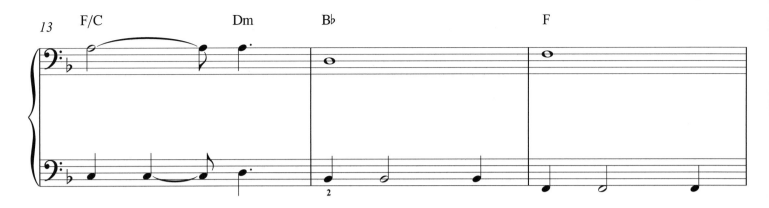

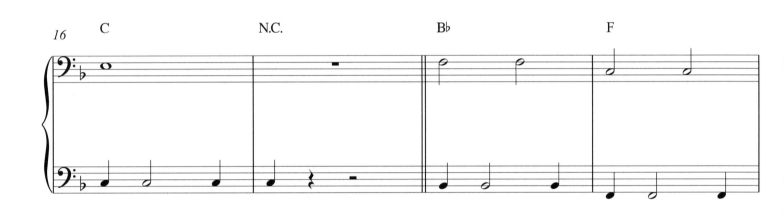

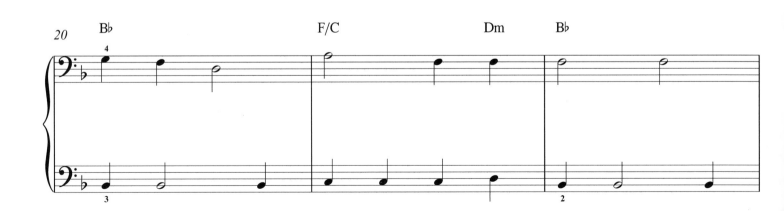

Primo

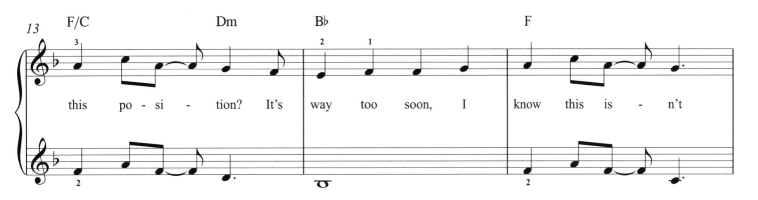

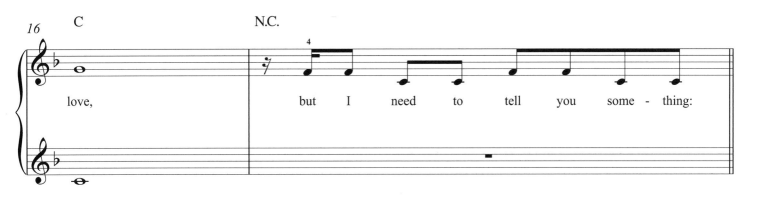

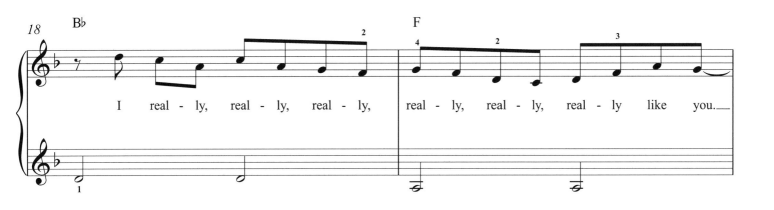

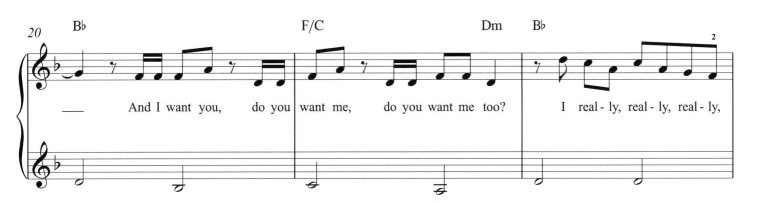

Secondo

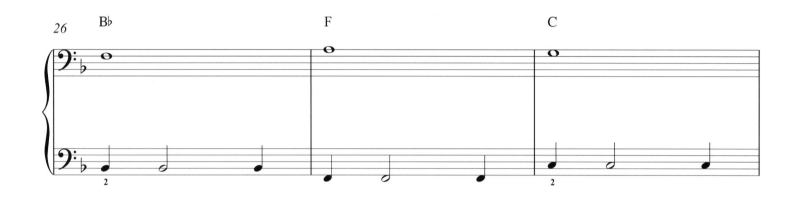

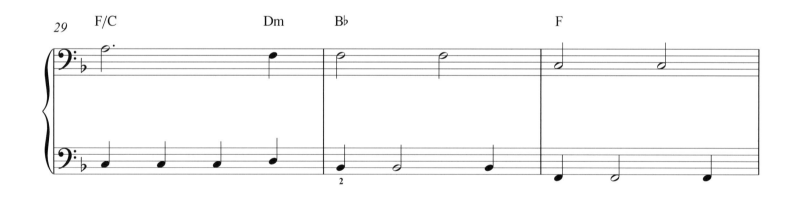

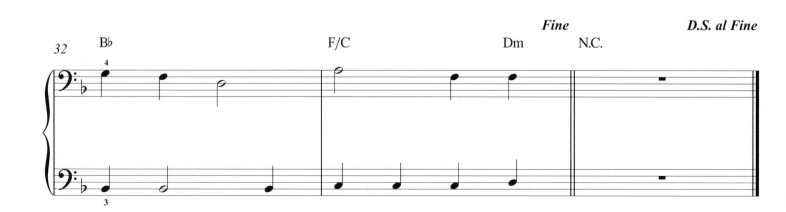

Primo

real-ly, real-ly, real-ly like you.___ And I want you, do you want me, do you want me too?

Oh,___ did I say too much? I'm so in my head when we're out-

-ta touch. (Out - ta touch!) I real - ly, real - ly, real - ly, real - ly, real - ly, real - ly like you.___

Fine   **D.S. al Fine**

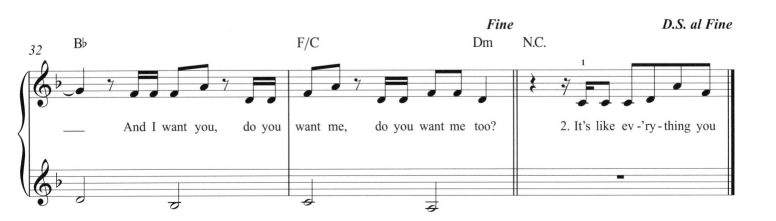

___ And I want you, do you want me, do you want me too? 2. It's like ev-'ry-thing you

55

Secondo
Let Her Go

Words & Music by Michael Rosenberg

'Let Her Go' was a huge international smash hit for Passenger, topping the charts in 21 countries including Australia, Ireland, Italy, Germany and Sweden, reaching No. 2 in the UK and No. 5 on the US Billboard chart. It was released as the second single from Passenger's third album *All the Little Things*.

Primo

Let Her Go

Words & Music by Michael Rosenberg

Hints & Tips: This song is quite soft throughout, so try and play with lots of expression. Don't let the second-part crotchets become too heavy.

Secondo

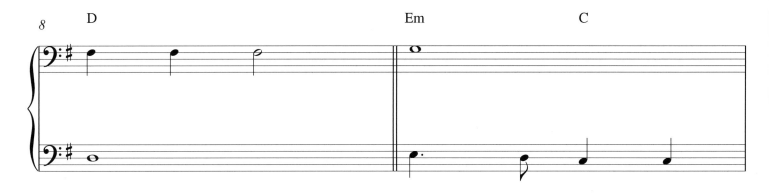

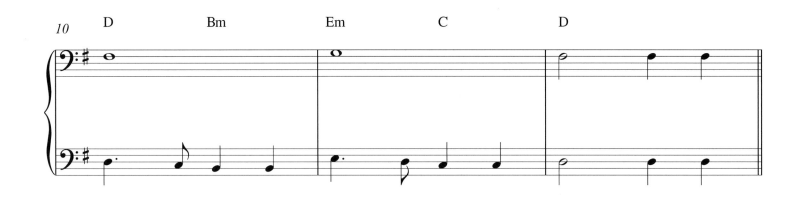

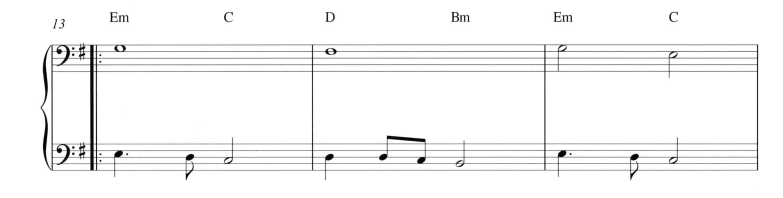

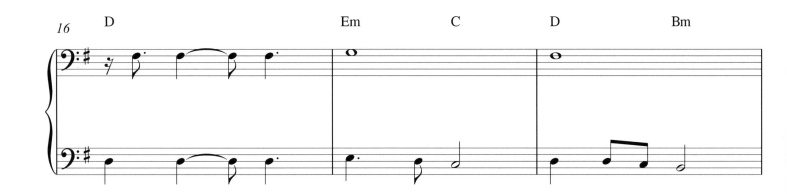

Primo

Secondo

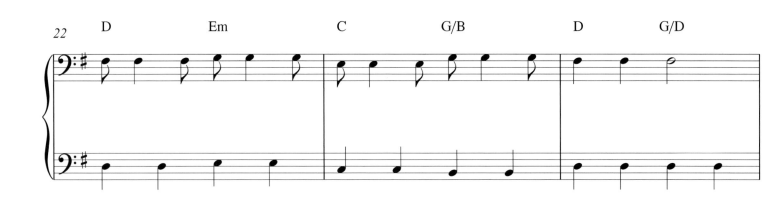

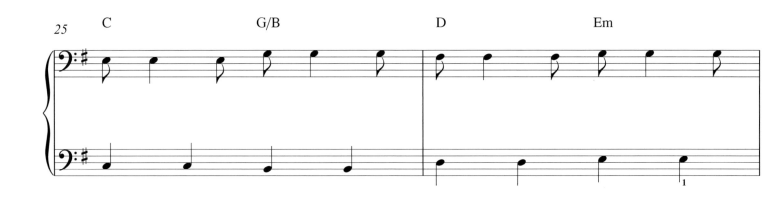

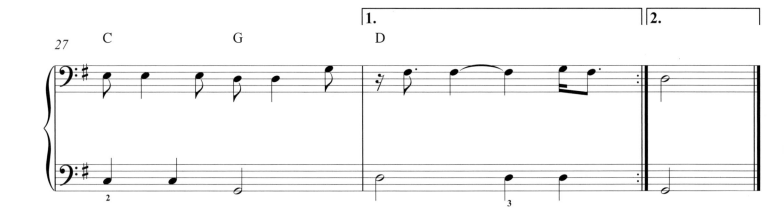

Primo

61

Secondo

See You Again

**Words & Music by Justin Franks, Cameron Thomaz,
Charlie Puth & Andrew Cedar**

This heartfelt hip-hop track forms part of the soundtrack to the tearful final few minutes of *Furious 7*, which is a tribute to the late actor Paul Walker, who passed away while working on the film. The song hit a personal note for many involved as well as fans of the film franchise, with the uplifting track being seen as a very fitting tribute to a beloved actor.

Primo

See You Again

**Words & Music by Justin Franks, Cameron Thomaz,
Charlie Puth & Andrew Cedar**

Hints & Tips: There are some high passages in the right hand of the first part. Work out any notes you're unsure of before you try playing through, marking them on in pencil if necessary.

Secondo

Take Me To Church

Words & Music by Andrew Hozier-Byrne

'Take Me To Church', the debut song from Hozier's self-titled debut album, was nominated for Song Of The Year at the 2015 Grammy Awards. Its lyrics are about comparing love to religion, and express the singer's frustration with the Catholic Church's stance on homosexuality.

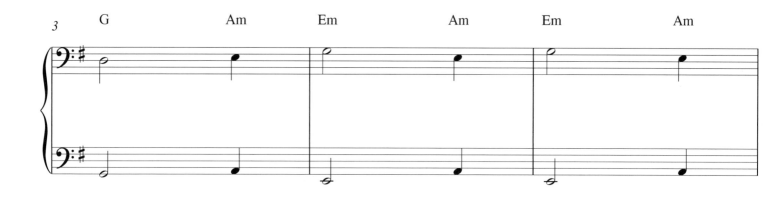

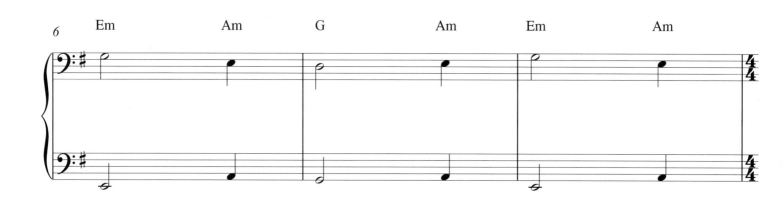

Take Me To Church

Words & Music by Andrew Hozier-Byrne

Hints & Tips: There are a few time signature changes in this. Play through these passages to make sure you both have the timings right.

Secondo

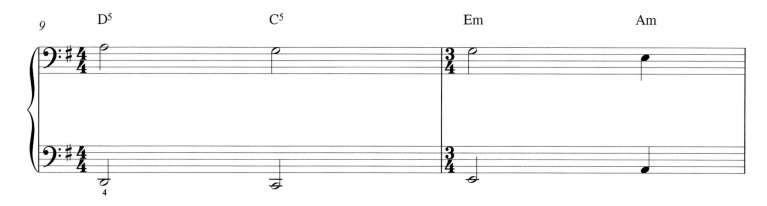

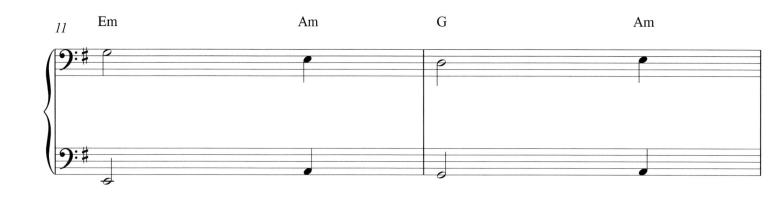

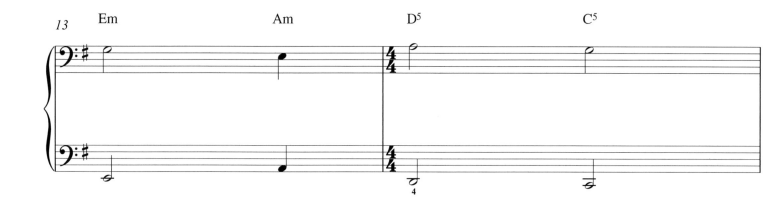

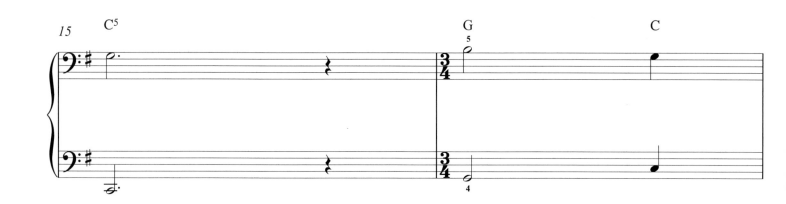

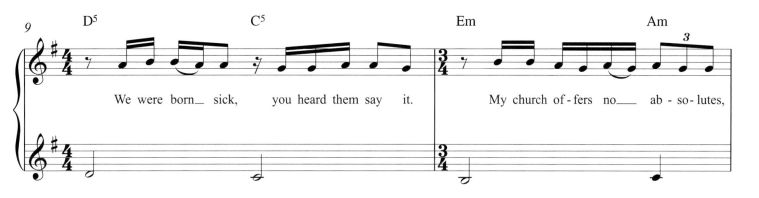

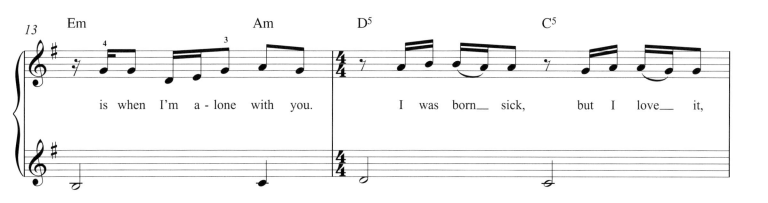

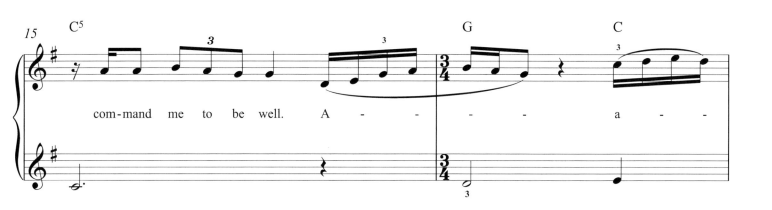

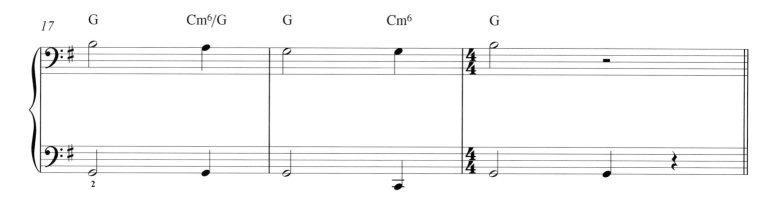

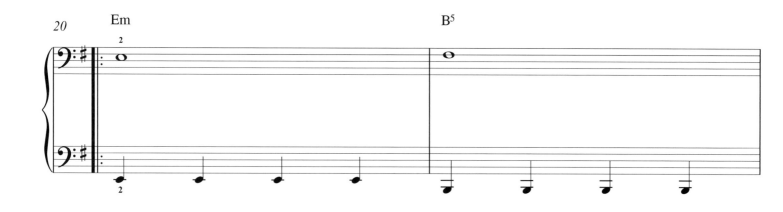

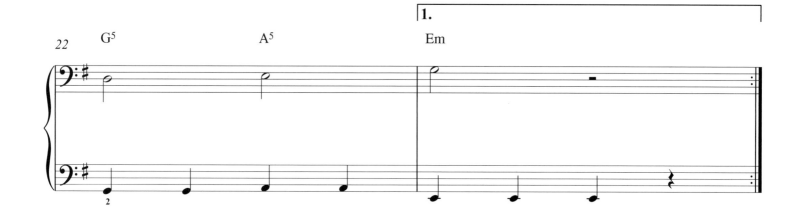

Primo

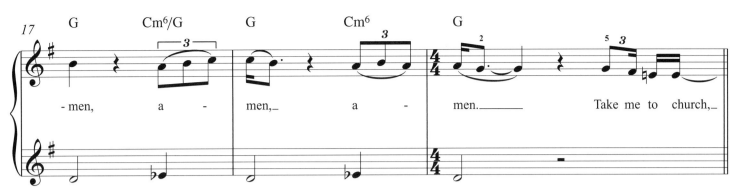

69

Secondo

Thinking Out Loud

Words & Music by Ed Sheeran & Amy Wadge

Sheeran famously wrote 'Thinking Out Loud' using a guitar gifted to him by Harry Styles of One Direction, yet piano features heavily on this steady-paced ballad that celebrates the enduring quality of love and romance. It was one of the last songs to be written on the album *x*.

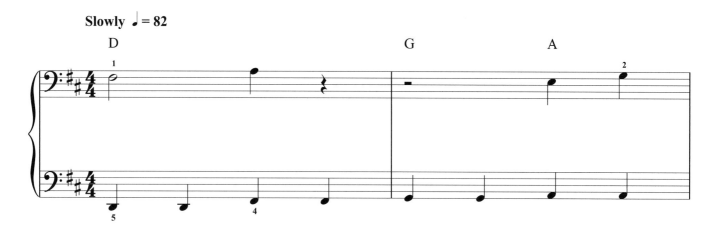

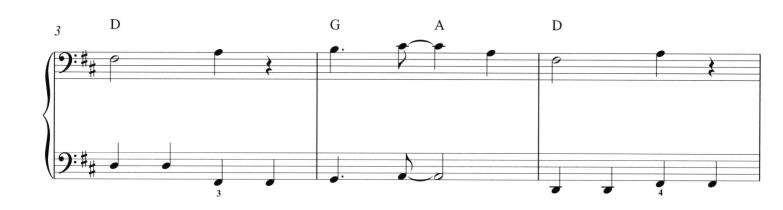

Primo

Thinking Out Loud

Words & Music by Ed Sheeran & Amy Wadge

Hints & Tips: Practise bars 33 and 34, both parts, until they can be played with confidence – these need to be precise and together.

Secondo

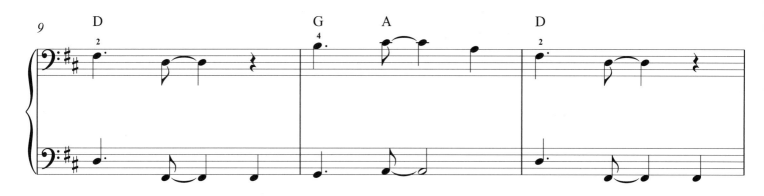

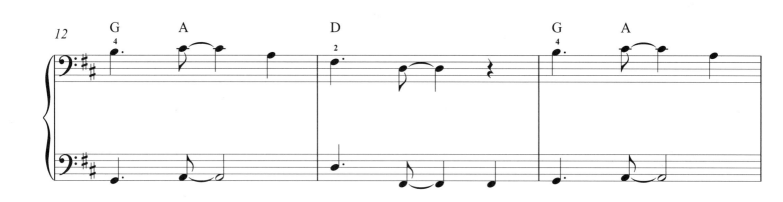

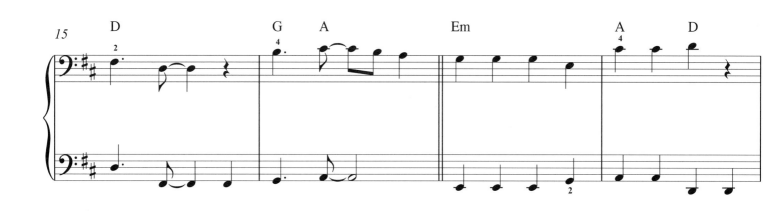

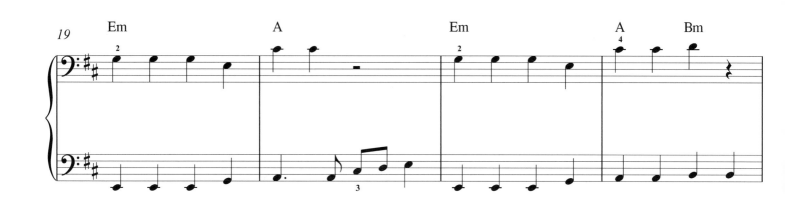

Primo

73

Secondo

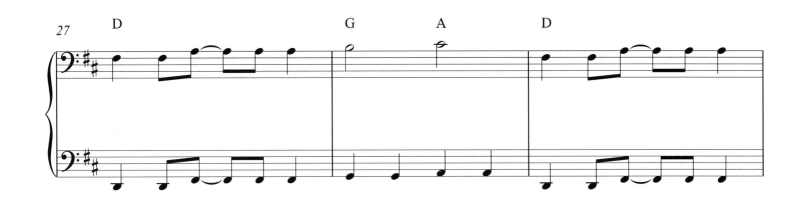

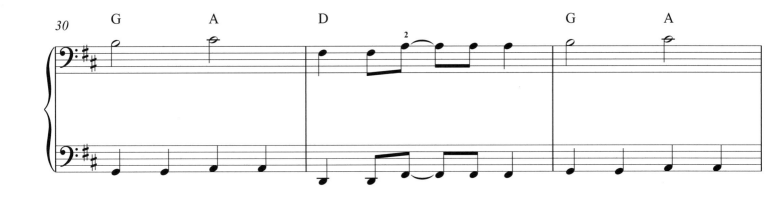

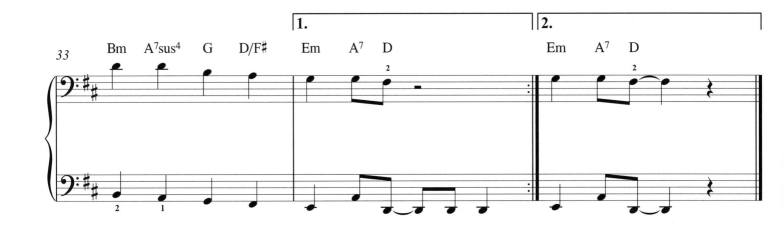

Primo

75

Wildest Dreams

Words & Music by Taylor Swift, Shellback
& Max Martin

The fifth single from Taylor Swift's fifth studio album, *1989*, 'Wildest Dreams' is an atmospheric romantic ballad. The video was filmed in Africa and stars Swift and Scott Eastwood – son of Western-movie legend Clint Eastwood. The title is repeated eight times throughout the song!

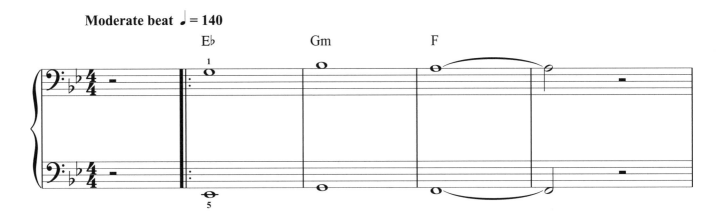

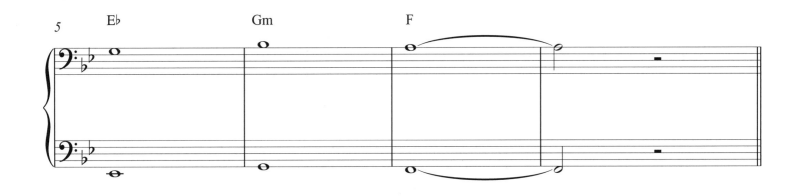

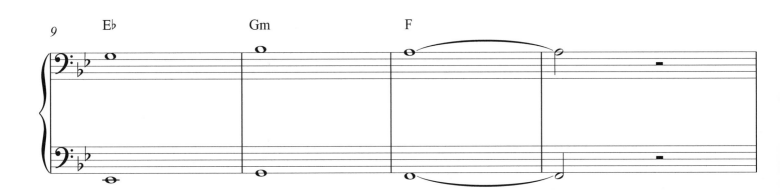

Wildest Dreams

**Words & Music by Taylor Swift, Shellback
& Max Martin**

Hints & Tips: Keep the left-hand of the second part light when it comes to the chorus in bar 17, keeping it slightly bouncy so it doesn't sound too heavy.

Secondo

Wings

Words & Music by Ryan Tedder & Jasmine Van Den Bogaerde

'Wings' was the lead single from Birdy's second studio album, *Fire Within*, and was co-written with Ryan Tedder, who has collaborated with Beyoncé, Adele, One Direction and Taylor Swift – to name a few! Though it was originally released in 2013, this song saw a return to the charts following its use in the Lloyds Bank 250 year anniversary advert.

Wings

Words & Music by Ryan Tedder & Jasmine Van Den Bogaerde

Hints & Tips: Keep both parts soft throughout. There are a few stretches in the right hand of part one, so check the fingering carefully.

Secondo

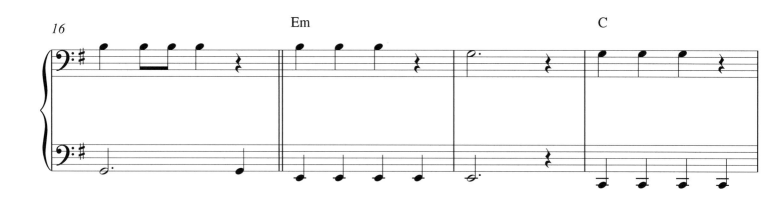

Secondo

Writing's On The Wall

Words & Music by James Napier & Sam Smith

Taken from the highly-anticipated 24th Bond film, there was some debate as to who would sing the theme song for *Spectre*. Sam Smith's 'Writing's On The Wall' was released as a digital download on September 25th 2015, one month before the world premiere of the film. The song became the first ever Bond theme to reach No. 1 on the UK Singles Chart.

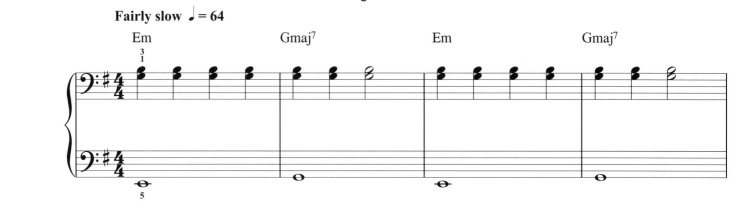

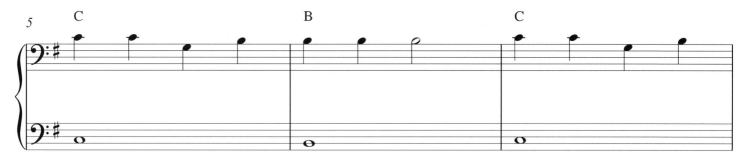

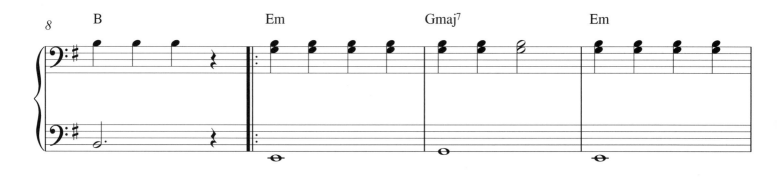

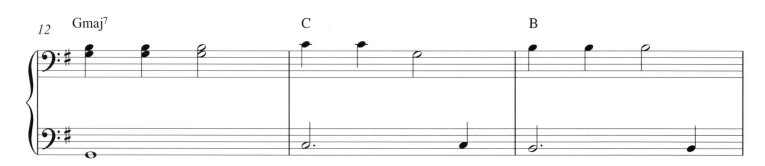

Writing's On The Wall

Words & Music by James Napier & Sam Smith

Hints & Tips: Keep the chords in the second part soft, underpinning the melody in the first part. Try to play as expressively as you can, perhaps experimenting with adding your own dynamics!

Secondo

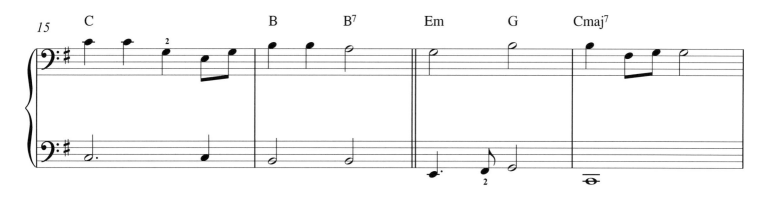

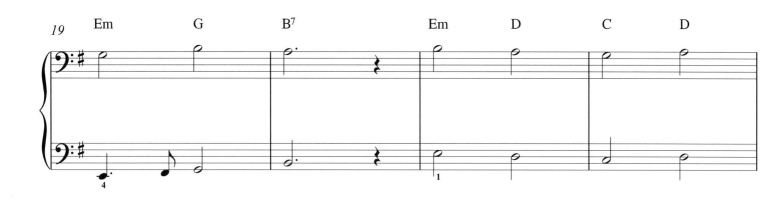

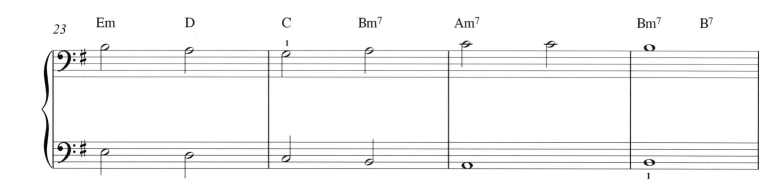

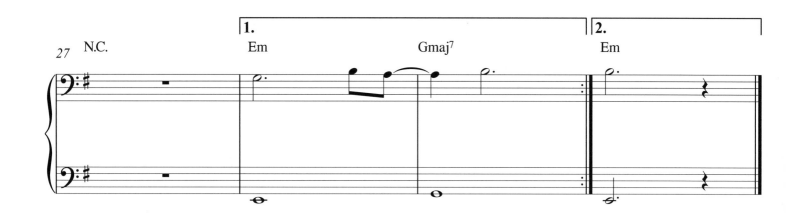

Primo

no more use in run-ning, this is some-thing I got-ta face.
hope be-gins to shat-ter know that I won't be a-fraid.

If I risk it all could you break my fall? How do I

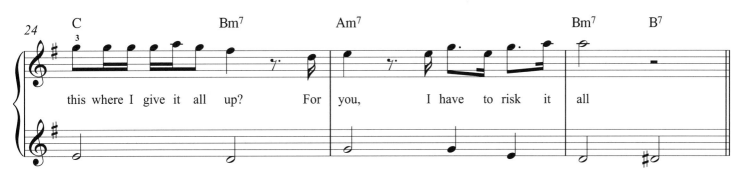

live? How do I breathe? When you're not here I'm suf-fo-cat-ing. I want to feel love run through my blood, tell me is

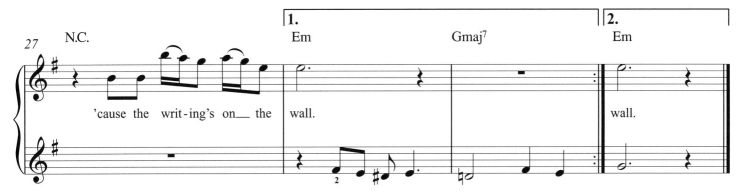

this where I give it all up? For you, I have to risk it all

'cause the writ-ing's on the wall. wall. wall.

123456789

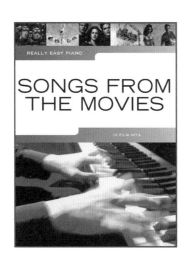

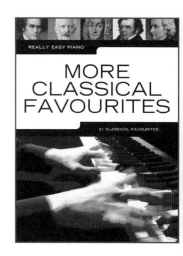